with all good
New Year

MW00674310

Ellison Smyth

Chips and Shavings —
More Stories by
Ellison Smyth

Illustrated by Joni Pienkowski

Pocahontas Press, Inc.
Blacksburg, Virginia

Chips and Shavings — More Stories by Ellison Smyth
by Ellison A. Smyth
Cover Design and Illustrations by Joni Pienkowski
Other contributions by John Kline, Gentry Studio of Blacksburg,
    and by Dr. Gavin Faulkner, Rowan Mountain, Inc.,
    Blacksburg, Virginia.
Printed and bound in the United States of America by Common-
    wealth Press, Inc., Radford, Virginia, U.S.A.

© 1997 by Pocahontas Press, Inc., Blacksburg, Virginia, U.S.A.
    All rights reserved. No part of this book may be reproduced in any
form or by any electronic or mechanical means including information
storage and retrieval systems without permission in writing from the
publisher, except by a reviewer who may quote brief passages in a review
to be printed or broadcast. Contact Pocahontas Press, Inc., P.O. Drawer
F, Blacksburg, VA 24063-1020.

First Printing 1997
ISBN 0-936015-67-5

Library of Congress Cataloging-in-Publication Data:
Smyth, Ellison A., 1903–
    Chips and shavings — More stories by Ellison Smyth / Ellison
    A. Smyth
        p.   cm.
        ISBN 0-936015-67-5 (pbk)

To Family and Friends

With love and appreciation

A Note from the Publisher

Chips and Shavings is a second collection of essays by Ellison Smyth, following his best-selling *RetroSpect*, published in 1993.

The essays in both books were first written for and presented to the Warm Hearth Writers Workshop, a creative writers group led by Nikki Giovanni at the Warm Hearth Retirement Village in Blacksburg, Virginia.

Ellison and Mary Linda Smyth are a legend in Blacksburg, for bird-watching and gardening, for leading the community (not just the Blacksburg Presbyterian Church) in human rights activities, and for their warm and loving personalities. All who have known them, all whose lives have been touched and bettered by their presence in the world, all who appreciate a kindly look at human behavior and foibles — in fact, all of us — will enjoy reading these comments by Ellison on his — and our — human lives.

Mary Holliman
November 1996

Contents

Chips and Shavings

as told by Ellison Smyth
to Susan Smyth Lindenberger, May 3, 1996

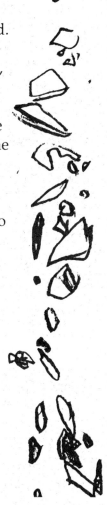

The first woodworker I know of in our family was Alexander "Sandy" Allan from Wick, in Caithness, Scotland. Colonel Memminger, later Secretary of the Treasury for the Confederate States, brought Alexander Allan over from Scotland to do cabinet work at his summer place in North Carolina. Uncle Ellie (Captain Ellison Smyth) bought the place from Memminger after the war and named it Connemara; he owned it for 50 years. Carl Sandburg's family later bought the estate and donated it to the Park Service in memory of Sandburg, who actually had nothing to do with the place.

The bookcase in the living room at Blowing Rock is Sandy Allan's work. It used to stand against the stairway in Grandmother Allan's home at 222 Rutledge Avenue in Charleston. The walnut drop-leaf desk which Mother used and is now Allan's is also Sandy Allan's work.

With five children, my mother decided she needed a cow. Father said, "Perish the thought." So we got a cow

1

from John Huston, who lived on the hill where the water tank used to be. The cow was named Sukey.

Father said we had to build a barn for shelter and to store hay. So that's when he got out his saw and hammer — he was handy with tools. He got some scraps of lumber, freshly sawed, and I learned how to drive a nail straight. That was my first experience with wood working: nailing siding on a cowshed. Next we built a two-story lean-to for the hay, with a hinged door for throwing the manure straight onto the garden — very handy.

Father had permission to cut the alfalfa and rake hay from Mr. Matthews, Supervisor of Buildings and Grounds at VPI. He used a long scythe to cut the hay; I still have the scythe stone for sharpening it. We'd let it cure a couple of days. We used a baby carriage with big wire wheels — built a hay frame to go over it and used that to haul the hay to the barn.

Our pony Crescent never could go faster than a slow walk. We'd hitch Crescent to the hay frame and finally get him moving. He pulled that carriage to the hay barn window, and we'd throw the hay in. It was as high as a man could reach with a pitch fork. Someone — usually me as low man on the totem pole — stood inside to pull the hay in and pack it down. One place I learned to hate cows was in that hay barn on a hot summer day. The other was morning milking when it was below freezing.

When I was about twelve, we built the Aladin Cottage on the Salem farm. Cousin Alec Allan would come up from Carolina to play with the mountain cousins. We boys slept in a tent in the alfalfa field. One of the mountaineers, Mr. Coleman, lived on the

Ellison at 8
w/ hammer

road to Twelve O'Clock Knob above us; he took charge of putting the cottage together.

Jake Blankenship was tenant on the farm. He could do anything. Jake had two small children and wanted them to have a better chance in life than the little cove where he'd grown up. Jake milked the cow and looked after the place. He got $50 a month and all the produce he wanted from the garden. Jake taught me how to carve peach-stone monkeys, like all you children have.

During World War One the town tried to come up with something useful for the Boy Scouts to do, to give them a feeling of participation in the war effort. Black walnut is the classic wood for gun stocks: it's solid, doesn't warp or check, and holds its color. So they asked the Scouts to locate all the walnut trees in the Blacksburg area.

I chose Smithfield: I knew where every walnut tree in the Smithfield area was. Recently, I found an old notebook cataloguing each tree, giving its location and dimensions. Only a few were cut then, and the logs left lying on the ground.

After I started wood working, almost fifty years later, I got hold of those old walnut logs. Some of the walnut furniture I made, like your desk, was made out of those logs. Several of the trees were cut later; not all of them were from World War One.

There are a couple of sinkholes at Smithfield where they'd quarried for rock. A big walnut grew in each of those sinkholes. Henry Mosby devised a way to rescue those Smithfield trees and got someone to haul them to the old county sawmill. Henry and I competed for those walnut boards. I traded him some

L. Pienkowski

CARYING a PEACH-SEED MONKEY

5

cherry for walnut lumber. The wide boards for the bottom drawers of the walnut desks came from Henry Mosby.

Dick Howerton, the Baptist minister, was a good friend. We had a lot in common. He had made all their furniture when he had a church in the Lumberton area of North Carolina. I was fascinated and envious and determined to learn how to do it.

I learned how on his shopsmith. Then I got one from a fellow who lived in a row of houses below Palmer Hill; got it for $200. Later it was used at Warm Hearth in the wood-working shop. It was a lot of fun. The mark of a good woodworker is that he has all his fingers. A saw doesn't ask any questions. You have to be very careful.

Dick started having spells of depression. The doctor prescribed more time on his hobby. Sarah Howerton would phone me: "Dick's feeling down. Can you come up to do some wood work?" So I'd phone Dick with a problem on one of my projects, and we'd get together. It was mutually beneficial. We'd get together about once a week, do wood work, and chew the fat. That's how I really got started on wood working.

Mountain Man

He was a real mountain man, from
"t'other" side of the Knob on Back
"Crick". He did not talk much, and
when he did, it was the Elizabethan
English of the Southern Appalachians
— mellow, laconic, and with a sugges-
tion of the 1611 King James Biblical
picturesqueness. His wife was from the
same section and vintage. They had a
small boy and a smaller little girl. They
came looking for a place where they
could raise the children with some of
the advantages they never had. Jake
agreed to be the tenant on a little apple
orchard and farm my father had bought
as a suitable place for later retirement.
This place was a mile east of the town of
Salem on a foothill of the knob, with a
beautiful view of the Roanoke Valley.

Jake had hands as big as hams, and
yet he could do the most delicate kind
of work, like making a fiddle that you
could really play. He taught us kids to
carve peach seed monkeys, and made
wonderful toys, like trucks, steam
rollers, and saw mills, out of old tin cans
and whatever scraps he could pick up.
He made a woven bailing wire basket
for measuring out the oats. It was so

heavy I could hardly lift it as a boy. He had the strength of an ox. He did not even grunt when he picked up a 165-pound barrel full of apples, holding it between his hands, and set it up in the wagon. We never heard him raise his voice, either correcting the children, or getting the team of horses to do what he wanted them to do — and what they didn't want to do. But he got action. In the hay field when other men timidly poked a pitch fork part way into a pile of hay, he just rammed his fork down through the top of the hay cock and picked the whole thing up at once and loaded it onto the hay frame. He loved to plow and plant corn on the ten-acre field below the orchard.

There were about 35 acres of apple trees — stayman, pippin, winesap, York, grimes, golden and a few other varieties. Also an acre of peaches, a hundred yards of grapes — Niagara, Concord, and Delaware reds. A mile up the hollow we had 140 acres of mountain land, with two little streams. When Jake first came, the only way they could get water was to go down a rather steep hill to the dry run creek bed, where a barrel had been sunk near the edge of the run, and good clear water could be obtained. Jake had to carry buckets full of water up the hill to the small tenant house. When it was agreed that a well should be drilled, Father knew exactly where he wanted them to drill, but Jake insisted that he knew a good "water witch" who could locate a place where there was bound to be water. This man would do it for fifty cents. In order to satisfy Jake, it was agreed for him to contact his "water witch" from Back Creek. The man came with his forked switch — either willow or witch hazel — and walked back and forth in the yard, and his switch always turned in his hands right at the place that had been marked by Father as the most convenient location with respect to the house and the barnyard. The "water witch" was pleased to receive his fifty cents.

Soon the well driller was at work — much to the edification of us children. At about seventy-five feet a good stream of clear, sweet water was struck. A housing was built, and the next step was to provide a tank and a small gas engine to operate the pump. Jake took us with him up on the mountain where he located four good locust trees and brought back the long logs on the wagon frame. It was quite exciting watching them erect the frame and put a 500-gallon metal tank on the platform about 15 feet above ground. All this took several years to accomplish, but was a great help to our tenants. In the meantime, Jake had built a very nice lean-to room at the back of the house for kitchen and storage.

One day he invited us to go up on the mountain to capture a swarm of bees, and rob the bee tree. This was interesting and exciting. At the creek bees would come to drink, and Jake would watch where they went — in a bee-line to their tree. We followed. Jake located the tree. He told us to stay at a safe distance, while he put on his veil and gloves and took his axe and cut the tree. After splitting the tree, he scooped up a bunch of the bees that were clustered around the queen, and put them in a frame he had brought from one of our hives. Swarms of bees followed the ones around the queen. Jake scooped out a couple of buckets full of honey and comb. We followed at a safe distance behind the wagon on the way home. Bees were very important as pollinators for the apple orchard, so Jake added his new hive to the three or four already near the yard. Several years later, after the folks had built a big house in place of the campsite where we used to spend the summers, Jake brought over a whole wheelbarrow loaded with supers full of honey, and a swarm of bees like a cloud followed him. We children sat on the back steps and cut the honey comb out of the supers and packed the one-pound squares full of honey into crocks and jars — to eat and to give to friends. The bees were not interested in stinging us, they were just eager to get their honey back. When we licked our fingers, we had to be careful not to inhale a bee.

As you can see, Jake was a very versatile person. They had to be, back on t'other side of the knob, where they had to make do or do without.

Jake had a big garden, where his wife did most of the work, but he had free use of all the apples, peaches, and grapes they could use or sell at the farm market in Roanoke. He would take a wagon load of stuff to market, and Saturdays were great days there. His wife also had jars of jelly and apple butter which added to the stipend he received as a tenant and, with their frugal living, they made out very well.

Jake told us that his great grandpappy used to go across the mountains to some place to get lead from a mine to make bullets to keep "b'ars and Injins" from raiding their place in the cove off Back Crick. I do not believe that Jake would ever have needed a gun to keep such critters away from their cabin.

Ferry, or "The Fairy Boat"

(according to our children)

It was an old side-wheel paddle boat that ran from its pier near Adger's Wharf on the Cooper River in Charleston, South Carolina, to a dock on Sullivan's Island. That dock was the ferry's terminus — but the beginning of the trolley line that ran from there the full length of Sullivan's Island, then across a short trestle and almost the full length of the Isle of Palms. What fascinating memories those words conjure up for a "hillbilly" boy from Blacksburg.

We were visiting Grandmother, Mrs. James Allan on Rutledge Ave. Grandmother's coachman would drive sister Amey and me — and usually a couple of Allan cousins, Alec and Susan Allan. Grandfather James Adger Smyth still had the old Adger cottage on Sullivan's Island where, as a boy, my father remembered tales of the flagships of the Adger Line doffing their colors as they passed the Adger cottage on their way to the ports up and down the Atlantic coast. Some even crossed to Liverpool. Fort Sumter was in ruins from the Confederate shelling when Lincoln had tried to reinforce the garri-

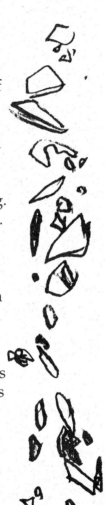

son there, leading to the outbreak of the Civil War.

I was not interested in such world-shaking events then, but on board the old ferry — a side-wheeled paddle ship — this small country boy from Blacksburg was fascinated by the smell of hot oil on the machinery, as I watched the moving of the "walking beam," as it was called, that connected the cranks that operated the side-wheel paddles. The smell of the hot machinery and shipboard and that of the pluff mud on the land side and the fresh sea breeze to sea-ward, was a good introduction to the excitement of watching the docking of the ferry at the Sullivan's Island terminal. And this was just the introduction to what was to follow. We went through the gate at the dock to the trolley cars. These cars — usually two or three connected together during the summer season — ran the whole length of Sullivan's Island and then crossed on a trestle to the Isle of Palms and ran nearly to the Northern end of that sand bar. There were many summer cottages along the way and the train stopped often to let people on or off at the scattered beach houses or public beaches. As a boy I used to envy the life of the trolley conductor who got to ride the full length of the island twice a day.

My aunt, a single lady used to dealing with children of the Charleston area, had seen to it that I had on only a light cotton shirt and shorts. Aunt Amey left my sister and me to play at the beach cottage while she went down to a cousin's cottage to bring a couple of our cousins up to play with us on the beach and have a picnic lunch together. I was warned that the sun was too hot in the middle of the day to allow playing on the beach until later in the afternoon.

Looking out at the waves rolling up the beach —
an expanse of more sand than I had seen or imagined
could exist — was too much to resist. It was only
years later that I learned that five or six previous
civilizations that had been sun-worshippers had
perished and, although people of our day apply sun
block notions by the carload, people are slow to learn
and to heed.

Almost as soon as Aunty went to invite the cousins over, the lure of sun, surf, and sand was too strong
to resist. I went down and played, dodging the ebb
and flow of the waves on the beach, and then reveled
in building sand castles that melted away with the
coming of each wave. It was too fascinating to resist.
It was evening before it became evident that I was
going to join those ancient civilizations that had
perished from too much exposure to the power of the
sun.

I was too young and inexperienced to learn from
the regular denizens of the beach. The sand crabs
lived in their deep holes in the sandy beach until
night, before they frolicked on the sandy beach like
scurrying ghosts. The little fiddler crabs, when disturbed from their hiding spots, scurried with one little
claw upraised in mock defiance to another hiding
spot. The small fish and blue crabs left in the tidal
pools along the beach had sense enough to either
burrow in the sand, or just relax and wait for the next
tidal wave to refresh their pool or make a deep
enough exit for them to return to the sea.

Sister Amey, walking up the beach, returned with
a soft-shell dented golf ball that aroused Uncle
George at once. He asked if she could lead him to the

place where she found the funny ball. He was quite excited and got a cardboard box and followed her up the beach. Usually, Uncle George McDermid was quite lethargic. Theoretically, he was just a reluctant clerk in the hardware store until he had the chance to escape and go fishing. Amey's find excited him and he grabbed a cardboard box and asked her to take him back up the beach to where she had found the ball — which he said was a sea-turtle egg.

When they returned, they had about 140 turtle eggs he had grubbed out of the sand. They never get hard like chicken eggs, no matter how long you boil them. Uncle George would tear the soft shell, put in a pinch of salt, and slurp them down. When I tried it, I just got egg all over my chin. But I definitely formed the opinion that this was bad for the turtles, and it confirmed my leaning towards nature conservancy. This conviction grew all the stronger when Aunt Amey put turtle eggs in the muffins, grits, cocoa, and anything else she was cooking.

Uncle George McDermid, who had married one of my mother's older sisters, Aunt Jessie, knew all the waterways around Charleston, and it was said he could catch fish even when there weren't any. One day he took me in a rowboat along the waterways between the salt marsh and the back beach. We fished with hand lines over the edge of the boat. We caught a number of little sharks, stabbed them and threw them in to feed the crabs, and caught a number of crabs. We put the crabs in boiling water and, after they turned pink, we picked crab meat to eat with buttered grits for breakfast the next morning. They were delicious.

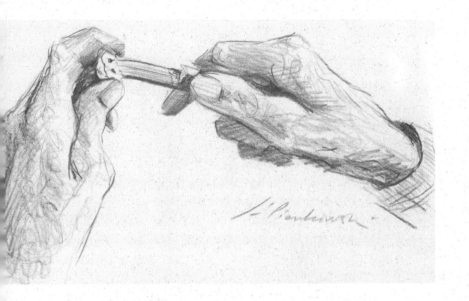

Tea-Hee

In the early 1900s forest fires frequently spread over Brush and Gap mountains. Some claimed they were purposely set in order to clear out the underbrush, so there would be a better crop of huckleberries. Sometimes the fires got out of control, and volunteers from the V.P.I. Cadet Corps were more than willing to get out of certain classes, like Thermodynamics or Differential Calculus, in order to go out and fight the forest fires.

From time to time a mountain cabin would be destroyed, and the people from Poverty Hollow would come to town begging food and clothing, etc. One of the large families, descended from Hessian mercenaries who had been employed by the British during our Revolutionary War, had 19 children. There had been so much in-breeding that a good man in that "tribe" was mentally retarded — or worse. One of these women used to come to our house begging for food — whether there had been fire or not. Mother always managed to scrape up something, and since her mother had come from England she always had plenty of tea — one of the props of the British social system.

After getting together some food items Mother asked the woman if she would like some tea. "What's that?" the woman asked. Mother explained how to brew it in boiling water, and gave the woman a little bag of tea. A few weeks later the woman came back begging food again. "But don't give me none of that there tea stuff." Mother was surprised, and, a little shocked, asked how she had prepared it. She was told: "I biled the stuff for about an hour like you done said, and thowed out the pot-likker, but the greens was too bitter to eat, so I thowed hit out too." No wonder the British couldn't win the war, especially with the aid of these Hessian mercenaries.

Some Early Founders of V.P.I.

Lyle Kinnear, in his magnum opus *The First One Hundred Years* gives quite a thorough account of the founding of the Virginia Agricultural and Mechanical College (in 1872; in 1895 more accurately named the Virginia Polytechnic Institute). He admitted that he was leaving it for others to fill in accounts of the people who really "fleshed out" and got the Land Grant college on its feet and going in the little, isolated frontier town of Blacksburg. I happen to be in a position to add a bit, and will do so in an informal way.

In 1891 Dr. John M. McBryde was called from the leadership of the University of South Carolina to re-organize the VAMC; and was given a free hand to staff the college. Some of the Virginia papers expressed outrage that he was bringing in a bunch of rice-eating South Carolinians instead of good FFV's. Others expressed satisfaction that at last a group of young well-qualified educators were called to head instruction, such as Smyth in Biology, Davidson in Chemistry, Sheib in English and Political Science, and two years later Pritchard in Physics and Electrical Engineering.

17

Ellison Adger Smyth is the one I was most intimately related to — he being my Father. A graduate of Princeton, with a Master's from Columbia University and work in law under Dr. Minor at the University of Virginia.

He was 28 years old, unmarried, and along with some other staff members lived in Number One barracks with the 135 boys. Each room had a fireplace, and occupants had to supply their own coal scuttle, wood box, basin, slop can, and water bucket. Out back there were the unheated privies, pile of Brush Mountain semi-anthracite coal from which you helped yourself, and a water hydrant connected to a tank in the cupola of the barracks, which was supplied with water pumped up by hydraulic ram from Stroubles Creek. Life was pretty well regulated by bugle calls. The town of Blacksburg numbered around 900 people. Being a Land Grant college, instruction in military science and tactics was required. There were periodic drills and military formations for class and meal attendance, church attendance (at the church of your choice), and any special convocations. The student body soon reached 300, and at the end of the era of McBryde's tenure in 1906 it reached around 700. All students had to be in the Cadet Corp. unless disqualified physically.

In such a setting, it was soon apparent that some outlets for physical activity, and cultural development, were necessary. At Princeton the subject of our sketch was familiar with the game of football. Smyth had sometimes played quarterback on the scrub team to give the varsity practice, though his real team sport was gymnastics. In 1892, he helped organize, and coached, the first football team at VAMC. John Stull was its first captain. They had to twist arms to get the boys to come for regular practice. The first game was with the St. Albans prep school on the edge of Radford.

Smyth used Walter Camp's manual and rule book. In his files I found a letter from Walter Camp answering some of his questions, of which I only remember one: "No, the ball carrier does not have to yell 'Down' when tackled, to end the play. If he is soundly tackled, he is down."

A Gym team was also organized. The students made the equipment: traveling rings, horse, parallel, and horizontal bars. For a shower they rigged up a sheet of tin with turned up edges — liberally punctured with nail holes, and put it over the rafters in a basement. To take a shower after exercise, you threw a bucket of water up on this tin sheet, scrubbed yourself vigorously and yelled for more water. Dean Sally Miles told me that when he was a student here (1897-1901) some of his fellow football players in the late 90s used to sell tickets to the country folks who always came to Sham battle, for a dime for admission to the museum; and then a big football player would collect another dime at the exit door before the people could leave.

Although Smyth only had one formal music lesson, he had a natural ear for music and through study mastered the intricacies of harmony. At both the South Carolina College, and here at VAMC, he played the organ for Chapel, led the Glee club, helped reorganize the marching band — playing the clarinet in both the band and orchestra. He played the organ at the Episcopal Church for two years, and after marriage, got back into his own church where he played the organ in both Sunday School and Church for twenty-five years in the Presbyterian Church. He was often called on by the YMCA Secretaries to give lectures on "Science and Religion."

Most of his time was taken up with teaching, and with collecting insects, birds, and botanical specimens. Lacking facilities for proper care at V.P.I., most of his insect collections (numbering some 25,000 or more specimens) are now in the Smithsonian Museum in Washington. His botanical specimens formed the original basis for the V.P.I. Herbarium, and his bird skin collections (also now at V.P.I.) form the nucleus of the Natural History museum.

Smyth served the Agricultural Experiment Station in many ways in its early days here. He eventually had an assistant, Horatio Stahl, who taught botany, and had various student assistants from time to time. Although without any regular secretarial help, he carried on a voluminous correspondence. He answered, often in long hand, questions from farmers and others, about insect pests and plants. As a custom from his legal practice in his uncle's law firm, he kept copies of his correspondence. Most of these are on file in the V.P.I. archives. He carried on a voluminous correspondence and exchange of Lepidoptera with entomologists all over the world (letters from, and to, England, Germany, Italy, Africa, Australia, Philippines, Borneo, South Africa, Canada, Mexico) as he built up his collection, now in the Smithsonian. His bird collection included 230 exotic hummingbirds, and over 1500 skins that he prepared with arsenic poison, and many of them mounted for exhibit in the museum he had in his laboratory. Smyth started the Herbarium with several thousand specimens he collected, identified and mounted. Over 1500 microscopic slides were prepared for his own research projects and for teaching purposes. He hand-colored many bird slides and was called on to give illustrated bird talks in South Carolina and Virginia. He opposed the bounty on hawks and owls and proved that they did more good than harm by examining the stomach contents and showing that they contained mostly the remains of rodents, not of chickens, as many farmers believed.

Of course anyone crazy enough to collect butterflies is regarded with suspicion. He used to comb the countryside during the 1890s — riding his bicycle. One day, returning from Poverty Hollow, where the argynis Diana and several smaller species were common, he caught up with a coal wagon from Slussers mine in Coal Bank Hollow. Walking up a long hill beside the wagon, the driver, seeing the butterfly net across the handlebars, asked: "Y-all been a' feeshin?"

"No, I've been catching various species of lepidopters."

"Bin a-doin which?"

"Catching butterflies."

"What in tarnation you doin thet fer?"

"It's connected with the way I make my living. What are you doing?"

"Delivering a load of coal to Mr. Price, cain't you see?"

"What are you doing that for?"

"Cause that's the way I make my living."

Well! Next day Harvey Price stopped in Smyth's office and said "Dean, I have a good one on you. Old Man Cook delivered a load of coal for me yesterday and asked me if I knew "one of them perfessors what catches bugs in a fish net — air he quite right in his haid?"

A V.P.I. Cadet in 1921

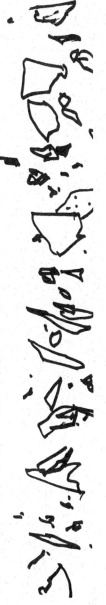

Every student at V.P.I. in the 1920s had to be in the Cadet Corps, unless physically impaired. Freshmen were called "RATS" and learned the following formula promptly:

(Sophomore) "Rat, what's the lowest form of life?"

"A Rat, Sir."

"Is there anything lower than that?"

"Yes Sir, a VMI Cadet, Sir."

Although I had spent my life on the V.P.I. campus, where my father founded and served as head of the Biology Department from 1891 to 1925, I was as "green" as any other rat when I entered as an engineering student in 1921.

We had the house at the end of the Faculty Row, next to the Ice Pond, which was flooded only in the winter to provide a skating rink. Thus, our house was on the edge of open country, and we were able to have a cow, a pony, ducks, chickens, turkeys, and during World War I, two pigs. I inherited the job as "Cow Boy" after my older brothers' graduation. Ever since then, my idea of Hell was having to milk a cow with a wet tail and sore tits, in fly-time.

Local cadets who lived at home were

subject to military discipline and had to serve their turn at guard duty and military drill formations. We kept our 30-30 caliber Springfield rifles, side arms, and other impedimenta in a designated room on the upper quad. Classes ran from 8 to 12 a.m., and laboratories and recreation in the afternoons. On Saturdays we had drill formations 11 to noon. Too often, on Saturdays the Bugle would blow "Inspection Formation", and we had to dash from class to don a dress blouse, cross belts, or side arms, grab our guns and hope they were clean, and fall in. I was a buck private in the rear rank of "E" company. There was no time to shine my heavy work shoes — usually stained with milk and other evidence of having been in the cow stable. The Captain of my company and Top Sergeant — with his pad, usually stopped in front of me and said, "Rat Smyth, you are the sloppiest man in my company. Can't you even shine your shoes for inspection?"

"Yes Sir, No Sir, I will, Sir." Five demerits!

That year Marshall Foch, Generalissimo of Allied forces in Europe during WWI, made a formal visit to America. Thomas Jefferson had served as Minister to France, so the Marshall made a courtesy stop at Monticello, then to Richmond on his way to Washington. Every military school and organization in Virginia went to Richmond to march in review in his honor.

The V.P.I. Cadet Corps was marched out beyond the then city limits. After several alerts the Foch cavalcade finally arrived. We presented arms, and then marched, platoon front, down Monument Ave. all the way to the Capitol at right shoulder arms. It is

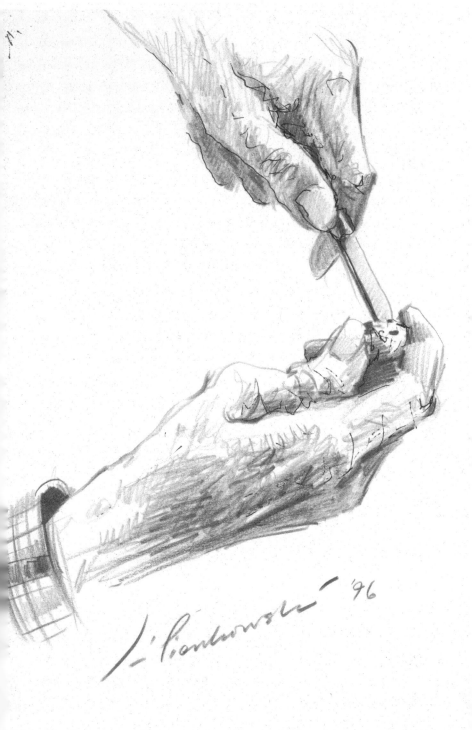

L. Piankowski '96

25

amazing how heavy a 16-pound rifle can get, and how cramped your arm becomes when you march too far, holding a straight line around the many monuments on that endless avenue. I lost any thought of ever following a military career.

My Junior year, I finally discovered that a clarinet did not weigh as much as a rifle, and transferred to the band. I never really learned to play the thing; but by then I had learned how to get out of some of the numerous drills. But when formal Government inspection came, every cadet had to be in the parade. The Captain of the Band knew from sad experience that I often blew sour notes on my clarinet, so he said "Smyth, put that thing in your mouth and wiggle your fingers, but for pete's sake don't you dare blow it."

Well, my Senior year I was able to return to civilian life!

Transitions

Having being taught, and believing, that although the ways of the Almighty are inscrutable, they are always right and good, my confidence in such faith was a bit shaken when the "hound of heaven" continued to yap at my heels. Why should I forsake a useful vocation for which I had been trained and had a natural aptitude? Such a change would involve the substitution of my engineering slide rule for an attempt to find the relationship of the Golden Rule to the study of Hebrew and Greek, the original languages of the Bible. Far be it from me to set my fallible human judgment over against the wisdom of the ONE whose will regulates the stars in their courses. Frankly though, I wondered if the Almighty had stripped His gears or blown a fuse this time.

However, with grave misgivings I accepted defeat and went to Union Seminary in Richmond and found that I was one of half a dozen "switch-backs" in my class from various vocations. With the wise and understanding counsel and instruction of some gifted teachers, and the pressure of having to study until several hours after midnight for academic preparation for each day and involvement in practical field work, I began to feel that maybe the Good Lord had more on the ball than I did.

Paired up with girls from the School of Christian Education, we visited in Hell's Bottom on Friday afternoons. This was the worst Black slum district in Richmond. There we found Black friends — not as potential domestics or unskilled labor, but as Christian friends.

But I still shuddered at the thought of speaking in public. Several of us took voice lessons to improve enunciation and voice strength and modulation pitch, and we accepted assignments to give Bible talks (we called them) during lunch hours. I had a Bible talk at the Carolina Bag Factory once a week, while a few brave and patient workers sat around on bales and boxes and ate their sandwiches and maybe listened. Or at the city gas works — which someone said was appropriate for me.

All this was a far cry from being Pastor of a church and having to preach every Sunday. One of our men had served as a summer supply parson under the then recently consolidated United Church of Canada, in Edmonton, Alberta. The idea of getting as far away as possible from anyone who knew me, when I started preaching, led me to apply for summer work in Canada. I received an appointment running from the first week in May to the middle of September in Saskatchewan in a village in the wheat country with a population of 101. Three of us got appointments for different parts of that province, which none of us could spell. We got permission to take our seminary exams early and to get back late in September. The office in Toronto sent me a ticket from Toronto to a flag stop named Khedive, Saskatchewan, and the price of my ticket from Richmond to Toronto. I wrote my folks that I would stop by home on the way back to Richmond in September.

At Toronto I found that my train was composed of about a dozen or so old day coaches full of central Europeans who could not speak English, a few Clyde Bank shipyard workers whose jobs had been closed, and a few Canadians from Nova Scotia who were seeking a better life by taking homesteads out West. It took this train two days to reach Winnepeg. It skirted around the northern side of the Great Lakes, which were still full of ice. When it stopped at villages on the way, many passengers dashed to the only store in sight to buy food, since there was no dining car. North of Lake Superior a man driving a dog team across a frozen lake was coming with mail sacks to put on the train from some place in the frozen North.

At Winnepeg, I transferred to a more Southerly route from Weyburn. The conductor looked at my ticket and said the train would not stop at Khedive, which was just a flag stop, unless there was someone there who wanted to get on board and set out the flag. However, the train would slow down enough for me to safely jump off running in the direction the train was going. The conductor said he would tell me when to go get on the step and when to jump if the train slowed down enough. The train did, he did, and I did — and landed on a cinder patch about twenty feet square. My footlocker had also been dropped off at the same place. There was no building, or other person there, but a sixty-foot tall wheat elevator on a side track gave some evidence of probable activity during harvest season.

A double row of unpainted houses flanked an open dirt road about two hundred yards distant. I left my foot locker where it was dropped and walked down to the nearest house and inquired for a telephone. I was directed to a house with a Post Office sign on it. Inside, I was warmly greeted by the Postmaster, who said he was Roy Muirhead, the Postmaster, and officer in the little Church and they were expecting a summer student supply parson. He told me that I could pick up my footlocker later — no one would touch it, and to come on, he would take me around to Roy Hunter's where I would be staying. Hunter was principal and teacher (with one assistant) in the little one-room school.

Mrs. Hunter welcomed me with a cup of tea and some scones. She showed me a little upstairs attic room with a cot, washstand and basin and pitcher of water and slop bucket. In that prairie country what passes as water is strongly alkaline, so that's one reason why they drink so much tea. While we were finishing tea, a pre-middle aged man stopped by and introduced himself as Scotty Buchanan, who was a salesman for a crop insurance company. He said he saw me drop off the train and figured I was their summer supply parson, and he hoped I played the game. Innocently, I asked him:

"What game?"

"Why, Mon, dinna ask a Scot what game — goff, man, goff."

This was a slack time of the year for him and for Art Best, who had charge of the elevator. They had rigged up a nine-hole course on vacant farm land nearby. They used empty tomato cans for cups, and had cleared off the weeds and filled a few gopher holes to make passable greens. Scottie said he could lend me an old mashie, a cut up ball, and one tee. He sported a weather-beaten bag with an assortment of clubs in various conditions, several balls, and a short-handled spade strapped on the bag. The spade was for digging his balls out of gopher holes in case they went astray. The air was filled with flying and crying curved-bill curlews. He said he actually hit one, in driving off one day.

Although I was familiar with the flat coastal country of the Carolinas, this endless flat prairie country was very different. Word got around quickly to members of the little church, and I hadn't been in Khedive 24 hours before Neil MacNeil came by and welcomed me and explained that the young summer parson was expected to get around to the farm members and others, and to visit for several days at each place, and participate in whatever work the family was doing. At the beginning of the second week in May, they were deeply involved in planting wheat, which was the life blood of the Province. MacNeil said he could use an extra hand, and since I was not going to be paid much for the summer work, I might like to lend a hand and earn some money.

In the 1920s, raw horsepower was used — few if any tractors were around. Every farm of one section (640 acres) had at least two dozen horses. They had to have big barns and haylofts. That far north in Summer it was daylight by 4 a.m. and it lasted until ten p.m.. Next day I started walking out to MacNeil's spread. A man driving an old Model T truck asked if I wanted a ride. I told him I was just going a couple of miles out to MacNeil's. He said distance fools you out in this prairie country — it's five miles from here to "Macs" — so I accepted his offer for a ride.

A six-horse span of big horses were standing hitched to a seed drill that looked like it was sixteen feet wide, and they were dumping a couple of sacks of seed wheat in it. I was told that they would let me have the privilege of driving that rig. It had sets of drills about two feet apart, and the seed would be covered by the discs mounted just behind the drills. The driver sat in a saddle above the discs. I was carefully cautioned that when I was bumped by going over a gopher hole, to be sure to fall behind the discs, because it would make too much of a mess if I fell off in front of them. Several trips to the end of the hun-dred-or-two-acre field had already been made by one of the boys, and I was told that the lead horse would follow the track of the previous one and all I had to do was to hold the reins, and at the end of the field one of the boys would be there to turn the team around. Sounded easy, but the feel of the raw power of six big horses in a span, and checking on the slower ones to keep them abreast of the lead horse, required a little dexterity. It was a fascinating experience, but I was glad I did not have to sit in the saddle all day.

The wild duck meat sandwiches that were brought out to the field for lunch, together with a bucket of hot tea, tasted mighty good. MacNeil said that when the slough was partially frozen, swarms of wild ducks practically filled the open water of the 1500-acre slough (pronounced slew) of "snow melt". MacNeil said just a couple of shots with his double-barreled gun gave them enough duck meat to last for a while. After cooking, the meat was separated from the bones and packed in canning jars, sealed with suet, and the jars were placed in the hurricane cellar for later use.

Dr. Sweet, the doctor, was a bachelor. Some of the people said he was a "snow bird." I never spotted him using dope. He often took me with him on his rounds. Regardless of what a person's ailments were, he invariably prescribed cod liver oil and sugar pills.

At church service one day, Omar Muirhead, brother of the Postmaster, who had been in the Canadian Expeditionary Force during World War One, and had been gassed, shell-shocked, and badly shot up, was sitting in one of the aisle side chairs. I noticed his shoulders twitching and his head bobbing up and down, and then he let out a yell and threw himself flat on the floor. Dr. Sweet called another man, and they just picked him up like a log of wood and as they carried him out, Dr. Sweet called back — "just go ahead, preacher, he does this all the time."

Then one of the women who had recently suffered a nervous breakdown started weeping and they carried her out. Then a young mother, , sitting with her infant on a front row chair, had to pick up her squalling baby, and they spent the rest of the service walking up and down across the back of the church, with the baby making appropriate squawks to encourage the preacher. Altogether, it was the most moving church service I ever attended.

Going with the doctor could sometimes be quite an adventure. He could be quite erratic in driving. In that flat country, he sometimes ignored dirt roads and swung his car unexpectedly across an open area, with the explanation that it was shorter to just cut across than to follow the road. On one such detour, he said he hit a wet spot and the car lost traction. He just got out, leaving the car in gear and started pushing, but his feet slipped out from under him and he fell down, but the car reached dry ground and went on without him. He knew that the car would travel in an arc, and he ran to the point where he figured he could catch the runaway. His comment was that this was just one of the hazards of the medical profession in those parts.

Every little village had its baseball team. There was considerable rivalry. Roy Hunter, the school principal, liked to play second base, so when Khedive's team played Pangborn, I kept school for Roy, or else covered what we called "roving field" — which usually meant that if the batter on the opposing team was fortunate enough to knock the ball beyond a base line, the roving fielder was supposed to get it.

The little one-room school presented some problems — or rather the kids did. One day I had to take a bowie knife from a kid who was trying to demonstrate how an Indian scalped his great uncle. Another time I was helping Roy with his chemistry experiment. It involved getting two of the older pupils to make sulphur dioxide from scratch. Sulfuric acid on iron filings. The experiment was such a success that we had to let all the kids have an extra long recess while we aired out the school.

One Sunday afternoon it became oppressively hot — black clouds covered the sky and the wind started howling. Roy yelled for me to grab a couple of pillows and hold them against the window panes just as golf ball-sized hail stones started pounding the house with a deafening racket. We saved the windows we cushioned with pillows, but every glass window in town on the windward side was broken, and shingles were literally chewed from the roof in many places. Four inches of ice covered the ground. Wheat fields that had had grain four feet tall three minutes before the storm struck now looked like they had just been harrowed. People were still raking up ice the next day to put in their ice boxes. The storm cut a swath three miles wide and sixty miles long. West of us a sheep herder got off his horse, put the saddle over his head and crouched to the ground. Six hundred of his sheep were killed — some had broken legs, and the eyes were knocked out of his horse. Neil MacNeil lost his entire crop for the second time in twenty years. He sold out and moved to Regina where he got a job as a carpenter. One German tenant farmer, who had taken out hail insurance, got a check for six thousand dollars cash, without the trouble of harvesting his crop.

One day Mr. Church, who ran the hardware and lumber store, got a freight-car load of rough lumber from Alberta. He could find only one man to unload it. Mr. Church said that since I was the only unemployed man in town, and could probably use the cash, he would give me eight dollars if I would help. The other worker was a big raw-boned German who could not speak any English. Some of the big 2 x 8 "splinters" — as he called them, were sixteen feet long and it took two men to handle them. It was an all-day job, and I earned my $8.00. The only German I learned was "nein", "danke schoen" and "bitte". I don't know if Hans learned any English except some carefully muted cuss words as I pulled out splinters.

In mid-summer, the days got really hot — up to 96 degrees F. But the nights were cool. When it rained, the black gumbo roads were a quagmire, and the mosquitoes came out in full force. Those friendly Diptera would be so thick we had to build smudge fires near each baseball player, and anyone who was crazy enough to stand in the batter's box couldn't see the ball coming through the cloud of mosquitoes. We just had to call off ball games on account of the pests.

By late August, the wheat harvest was under way. I went out to visit the Hugo Klitskis. They were a hard-working Swiss couple. We started reaping with a four-horse rig at 5:30 a.m. I picked up the sheaves and set up the stooks. Mrs. Klitski hitched up a second rig, after getting things in order to feed everyone for lunch, then renewed reaping until we stopped for supper. They had butchered the week before, so they had plenty of meat, potatoes, bread, and milk.

Every time a freight train came by from the East, a bunch of men would hop off to look for work in the harvest fields. Many were Scots from the closed shipyards on the Clyde. The Klitskis took on a couple of Polish immigrants. They were excellent workers and lined their stooks up in straight rows that made it easy for the stook loader to go down a row and dump the stooks into a hay frame driving alongside. In 1926, there were no combines operating in this country.

Threshing machines and their crews would set up in an area a big coal-burning engine with a big fly-wheel belted to the threshing unit. The spout delivered grain to high-sided wagons and these were pulled by teams of four horses and hauled to the wheat elevator. The straw and chaff were blown into a pile. One evening I counted over thirty rick fires on the horizon. That country is too dry to plow the straw under — it wouldn't rot before the next plowing season.

I spent a day helping Art Best at the elevator. The train had left several empty cars on his siding. The doors were boarded nearly to the top. The spout from the elevator was fastened to the top board across the opening, and the grain was poured into the car through the spout like water until the car was filled. When I asked Art how long he would have to wait for the engine to come and spout the next car, he said, "I don't bother with the engines, I will let you share a trick with me." We got behind the loaded car, put our backs against it, and with knees half bent, he said, "Put your hands on your knees and gradually straighten your legs." In that flat country, it did not take long to move the loaded car and push another into position. By evening, we had five loaded cars ready to be coupled to the next train. All night, long trains of cars loaded with wheat rumbled — either West to Vancouver, or East to Port Arthur on Lake Superior, to be carried on the ship canal through the Great Lakes and then to world markets.

People

Life is so full of interesting people — each with a story to tell. I pick one at random. Let's go down to Hell's Bottom. That was the common name given to the Seventeenth Street Black slum section in Richmond, Virginia, when I was a student at Union Theological Seminary. On Saturday nights the police had more calls to that section of the city than anywhere else.

Some years before I entered Seminary, a mission Sunday school and church started there and served by a resident Pastor with seminary students and young women from the Presbyterian School of Christian Education helping. When I entered Seminary in 1927, young men and women from these institutions visited the homes in the Seventeenth Street area in pairs every Friday afternoon as part of their field work. This arrangement sometimes led to more lasting engagements between students, and in most cases, led to a greater understanding of the problems faced by the Black community and to a deeper appreciation of friendships between individuals regardless of their differences.

We were always cordially welcomed in these homes and, after a brief visit, we were usually asked to read a passage from the Bible and have prayer with them. Often there was a sharing of problems and religious experiences. On the street where I usually visited, I always looked forward to seeing old Aunt Rebecca, as she was known by everyone. She was a

"GOD IS A SPIRIT,
INFINITE, ETERNAL, AND UNCHANGEABLE IN HIS BEING,
WISDOM, POWER, HOLINESS, JUSTICE, GOODNESS AND TRUTH"

real Saint. It always did me more good than I could ever have done this fine eighty-year-old friend. She had not only reared a large family of her own but was still taking in orphans and unwanted children — caring for them and imparting to them some of the fine virtues she possessed.

When we made these visits, we always carried several copies of the Gospels and Psalms. On one occasion, there was a small boy present when we stopped to see Aunt Rebecca. I asked him if he could read, and got an affirmative answer.

"Do you have a Bible?"

"No suh", he answered.

"If you will read from this little Bible, I will give it to you," I said.

His face brightened up and he eagerly opened to the first chapter of Matthew. He started struggling through that list of unpronounceable names in the genealogy of Jesus and then stopped and said: "These here BEGATS ain't the kind of reading they teaches us in school". So I turned to the second chapter and he started reading again: "Now when Jesus was born in Bethlehem of Judea in the days of Herod the King — " He smiled and said, "I've done heard this before."

I asked where.

He replied, "at the Sunday school on Seventeenth Street." So I wrote his name in the booklet and gave it to him with the admonition to keep going to the Sunday School.

One of the judges at the juvenile court in Richmond told the story of a Black boy who was brought before him charged with stealing. The boy said: "Before God, I didn't never steal nothing from nobody, never."

The judge replied "You said 'before God' — what do you know about God?"

The boy replied: "God is a Spirit, infinite, eternal and unchangeable in his being, wisdom, power, holiness, justice, goodness and truth."

The Judge said: "Son, where did you learn that?"

The boy replied, "at the Seventeenth Street Mission. "The judge said: "This case is dismissed. Son, keep going to that Sunday School."

Mountain Mission 1929

At the end of my second year in seminary, I served in mission work in the mountains of East Tennessee. There were five preaching points, with Sunday Schools and Vacation Bible Schools located in cabins, shacks, a store, and a school house. During the week I visited the cabins in the coves of "Po Valley," etc. The town church had promised me the use of a car, which was finally produced after we ran out of volunteer transportation. It was an old 1918 Chevrolet roadster. It had no windshield, no top, no brakes, no lights, no horn, and a screen-door hook kept the door partly shut. It was a hair-raising experience, navigating those mountain roads.

On one occasion, as I rounded a curve, I saw ahead a crowd of people in the middle of the road between two cars parked opposite each other. With no brakes and no horn — I just waved one arm over my head and let out the loudest Rebel yell heard since Appomattox. The people managed to scatter in time, and I came to a stop a mile down the mountain opposite one of the shacks where we held Sunday services.

Old Mr. Manus was always there on Sunday afternoons, and no one dared take his seat on the end of the front bench opposite a knothole in the wall. Mr. Manus was a dead shot with his tobacco juice. Instead of punctuating the service with a loud "Amen," he did it with an audible shot at the knothole, which he never missed.

On this particular day, old Mr. Courtney was sitting on a stump with a sack of corn meal nearby, resting. He lived up the mountain, so I asked him if I could give him a lift. He "lowed" as how he "mout" as well risk it, as he "were plum tarred out." He put his sack of meal on the seat and squeezed partly in, with his feet on the running board, and held on for dear life to the post that was holding up the windshield. We started up the "crick" bed. You ford the crick length-wise in those parts. We bumped from rock to rock, scraping bottom every now and then. We soon reached an "elbow" where I figured that by backing and pulling I might be able to turn around, and suggested we walk from there. Mr. Courtney lowed as how "no one had ever driv a car that fer up the crick befo." When we reached his cabin he pulled out a well-worn Bible and asked me to read and have prayer. He said no preacher had ever been up there before. He was a fine old man.

At another cabin I was shown real mountain hospitality. The man pulled a plug of "chawin terbacca" out'n of his "overhaul" pocket and offered me a chaw — "take as much as you can bite off." I 'lowed as how I didn't believe I'd chaw today. Then he offered me some "genuine home-growed burley twist" and an old, much used corn-cob pipe — but I 'lowed as how I wasn't much on smoking. Then the old woman pulled a box of snuff out of her bosom and said, "Ain't you goin to dip neither?"

They didn't seem to hold it against me for not indulging in the weed but just figured that some folks just didn't know how to live. It was beginning to get "dusky-dark," so when they offered me a battered old "rock ile" lantern to guide me over a twisting mountain trail out of "po valley" to the highway where my "transportation" was parked, I gladly accepted. They said they would pick up their lantern at "meeting" Sunday afternoon. They were fine, generous folks. Most of them had stills up the crick, but would not shoot first, if it was a servant of the Lord — not the law.

The Way It Was
Between World Wars I and II

Bill and I left Berlin on August 22nd, 1930, on the strasse "unter den Linden" in our five-horse-power Citroën. Since it was Bill's turn to drive, I just sat in the suicide seat playing Dixie on my German mouth organ.

As we passed one of the beer gardens, we could hear an American troupe singing "Crying for the Carolines" — (an old girlfriend of mine) — and at the stop light, "They Were Singing in the Bathtub."

Our little French Citroën then sped us on our way towards Dresden, by way of Herzberg. We reached this city on the evening of the 24th. According to our custom, we decided to spend Sunday quietly for rest, worship, and getting to experience a sample of the life of the place. We awoke in the morning with the sound of a brass quartet playing from the steeple of the church. We missed the worship service, but met the Pastor — young, intelligent, and enthusiastic about his work. He was a graduate of the University of Tubingen. He could speak about as much English as we could speak German. He brightened up when we told him we had been in Tubingen and that two of their famous professors, Karl Heim and Dr. Schlatter, had given lectures at our Seminary in America.

We walked around the town. It was a beautiful sunny day, and the lawns were covered with blue and gold flowers. We even got blue plum soup for lunch on a little side street. It was really very good.

When we asked, in our best German, what was going on — we could hear a band playing a marching tune. The man we asked said, "Oh, is it English you speak?" He was a carpenter and he and his wife had worked in Lawrence, Massachusetts, and would like to go back to America, but property they owned could not be profitably sold in Saxony now, at anything like its true value. He said Saxony had been taken over by the National Socialist people — their party, one of the 32 political parties, was using the swastika as their emblem. They were taking over the country, and were holding a big rally there that afternoon, with their leader scheduled to make a speech. The school children were all being lined up and would march in front. The men were wearing the official party uniform, which was supposed to be verboten, but because of the party's strength, was tolerated by the Hindenberg government.

While we were standing there talking with him, the parade started marching by. Men wearing a sort of brown uniform, with women and children in front. They stopped at the edge of a field where a "fussball" — soccer game — was going on. We watched the game for a while, and as twilight was coming on, we noticed that a bigger crowd was gathering around a very passionate speaker. Numbers were now leaving the game to listen to the harangue of the speaker nearby. Our knowledge of the language was insufficient to understand what he was raving about — but he was stirring up the crowd about something. Having heard Hitler on the radio a few years later, we had a hunch that it was Adolf that we heard that day in Saxony. He was more impassioned than any evangelist I had ever heard.

Snake Eyes

I served as Pastor of the Presbyterian Church in Hartsville, South Carolina, for seven years. The Manse was a big, two-story frame dwelling with high ceilings suitable for that climate, though in some places not too well sealed. A prominent lady was visiting with Mary Linda in the living room one day, when our five-year-old daughter Susan dashed into the living room in great excitement and cried out, "Momma! Momma! there's a snake in the dining room."

Wondering about the propriety of a little girl of her tender age seeing snakes, and in such an unusual place, Mary Linda excused herself for a moment to investigate. She returned a few moments later, quite unperturbed, to resume the conversation.

Of course the visiting lady wanted to know: "Was there really a snake in the dining room?"

"O, yes."

"What did you do?"

Mary Linda replied, "I picked it up and threw it out."

The visitor said; "Wasn't that dangerous ? — how did you know it wasn't poisonous?"

Mary Linda replied, "I just looked at its eyes. The pupils of a poisonous snake's eyes look like vertical slits — like a cat's. A non-poisonous snake's eyes have round pupils like a dog's."

The story got around Hartsville fast, and after that Mary Linda was introduced as the "lady who looks snakes in the eye."

After serving as a Pastor of the Blacksburg Church for 21 years, and having been retired for several years, I was asked to serve a three-month interim term back in Hartsville. After 25 years they still remembered Mary Linda as "the lady who looks snakes in the eye."

Watermelons

We lived in Hartsville for seven years before coming back to Blacksburg. This is just 12 miles from Darlington, which was then the shipping point for more, and bigger, watermelons than any other place in the country. Those big Darlington melons weighed around sixty or seventy pounds apiece. They were really beauties. They shipped melons out by the trainload, in cars and open trucks of all sizes, and in big farm wagons. They were shipped to all the big cities in the East. A big slice of Darlington County watermelon was featured as a special dessert in many of the famous restaurants and eating places in the country.

To help with harvesting and loading of the thousands of melons each year gave seasonal employment to hundreds of mostly dark-complected natives of Darlington. The big open-topped trucks full of melons usually had a Black helper sitting among the melons in the back of the truck. He would usually be advertising the delicious product he was presiding over by eating big wedges of melon, and, wherever they had to stop, he passed out samples of melon. Sitting there, like a king, eating all the melon he could hold — it was an enviable throne, until one time, a head-on collision wrecked the melon truck, and it was widely rumored that the Black boy riding on top of the melons was drowned in the juice of mashed melons. The newspaper story in the South concluded with the statement; "This was commonly regarded as a most glorious way to die — drowned in watermelon juice."

John Chavis

There are some Black heroes whose names and contributions to society are well known: like Booker T. Washington, George Washington Carver, Martin Luther King, Jr., Doug Wilder and Nikki Giovanni. There are many others that few have ever heard about.

In researching church records half a century ago I found mention of one I had never heard of, John Chavis. In the minutes of Lexington Presbytery under the date of October 1799 it is recorded that "John Chavis, a black man personally known to most of the members of the Presbytery, and of unquestionably good fame and a communicant in the Presbyterian Church, was introduced. Presbytery was satisfied with his practical acquaintance with religion, and they agreed, notwithstanding his color, to take him under the care of Presbytery as a candidate for the ministry."

At the Presbytery meeting at Timber Ridge, Va., November 1800, it is recorded that "Mr. John Chavis had not been able to prepare for his examination on the languages (Hebrew and Greek), and science, because of eye trouble. Mr. Chavis being a man of color, and as there is a prospect of his being peculiarly useful to those of his own complexion, Presbytery supposed his case something extraordinary, and therefore agreed to dispense with those parts of his trial, and proceeded to his examination on divinity."

For six years the Reverend John Chavis served as a missionary to his own people in Virginia and North Carolina; and in the latter state not only served those of his own color, but also ministered to white churches in Granville, Wake, and Orange Counties in North Carolina. He was widely known as an able and impressive speaker.

After Nat Turner's insurrection in Virginia in 1831, most of the Southern states placed restrictions on Negro preachers, North Carolina prohibiting them altogether. John Chavis then opened a classical school for white boys in Oxford, N.C. This school was patronized by some of the leading families in the state. Among his pupils were the sons of Chief Justice Henderson; W.P. Mangum — later U.S. Senator; and Charles Manly, later governor of the state. (Other events of his life are well documented. He died in 1838.)

An interesting postlude occurred in 1972 when ten blacks were arrested in Wilmington, N.C. for their "sit-in" protest against racial segregation at a lunch counter. Ben Chavis was one of the ten, who traces his roots to the Rev. John Chavis.

Mexico Safari No. 3: 1972

On the morning of February 21, 1972, it was a beautiful sight: the snow-covered volcanic peak of Mt. Orizabe 18,000 feet above us near Alvarada. This is in the orange and pineapple growing section. We got a ripe pineapple for about fifteen cents. At Catemaco we were directed to an open lot with no facilities, where we could park for the night for about a dollar.

We could walk along the shore of that beautiful lake. Two fishermen were casting their round nets and pulling in quantities of little silver white fish, which the natives eat raw — head, tail and all. They then smack their lips and declare them — "esta buena". We did not try them.

Next morning, we were up at 7:30. There was a light shower which pro-vided us with a beautiful rainbow. An adjoining field was covered with wild blue Ageratum with a backdrop of lush tropical jungle. There was not much variety in the butterflies — though I got a couple of iridescent blue skippers. They are the dickens to try to spread and mount. But the birds made up for the scarcity of Lepidoptera; Wilson's

53

warblers, red starts, brown jays, several varieties of hummingbirds, and red-billed fly catchers.

I had caught a couple of morphos there on our last trip, but this time they flew high and eluded my net. We pulled on down beyond a corn and banana plantation and, on the edge of the rain forest, a couple of careless iridescent skippers tried my patience when they got tangled in my net and I had to try to mount them.

Next day near Playa Hermosa we went over a very rough, bumpy road toward the celebrated, naturally carbonated spring at Cuyama. The man in charge insisted on our taking a cold bottle of Manzinit —naturally carbonated apple juice. It was very good, but we thought the tops of our heads would blow off with so much gas pressure. The man insisted on our each taking a big bottle and he wouldn't take any money for it — but wanted to see what we would do if we tried to drink it all. We tried to avoid drinking it all at once, but gave him all the "mucho gusto" and "buenas" and made our escape after downing about half a bottle. It was good, but too much of it and too much fizz.

Going on down the back road, we saw where they have been cutting out some huge trees. Mary Linda thought they were Cedro and Mastic. They were at least four or five feet in diameter. When we got back to our trailer we thought it would be a good idea to thoroughly debug ourselves and rubbed ourselves all over with benzine to kill any lurking bugs. Then we skinnydipped in the lake after lathering up. It turns surprisingly cool at night in the tropics. It was two-blanket cool in the trailer that night.

After breakfast next morning, we turned off the main road at Sihuarpan, where we took a short but rough road to El Salto, a truly magnificent waterfall. There we ate our sandwiches and, with the waterfall in the foreground and the tropical rain forest in the background, we relaxed. I did manage to catch two or three malachites (the beautiful green butterflies found in that part of the tropics). We then drove to the nearby village, and shopped at the native mercado. When we were invited to park for the night near the privy — surrounded with pigs, dogs, and naked children, we politely expressed our NO thanks and drove on further to an open field. We took a refreshing swim — skinnydip — and felt "mucho limpio". Spent a quiet night in the empty field. Next morning we saw that the field was surrounded with beautiful acassia and cockle sperman trees in full yellow bloom, and the roadside was fenced off with live gumbo limbo, and blooming mouse poison stakes that are alive marked the continental divide. From there to Tehuenta, we passed from the lush tropical jungle to an abrupt change as we started down the Pacific slope with nothing but cacti — a dry, arid section of the Pacific slope. The giant saguaro with its unpreached arms and the gray-topped Old Man Cactus all over the mountainside. It was an abrupt change. We saw some signs, reading — "Do not destroy the old men". That was some comfort to me until I learned that the gray-top cacti were called, appropriately, the old man cactus.

That will make a good stopping place; the Pacific slope has its own tales to tell another time.

Elusive Liguas

During our first four years in our new church facilities we were too financially embarrassed to put in the cables for the public address system. In consequence, I was knocked out for three months with paralyzed vocal chords. My doctor ordered me not to even whisper but to communicate by writing notes — and to escape some of the January weather by going to Florida for a couple of weeks.

We had been to an ideal, reasonably priced fishing lodge once before on Marco Island, before that West Coast naturalists' paradise was ruined by what the money grubbers call "Development". One of the regular patrons there from Wisconsin, had, over some years of wintering there, developed into a fair amateur malacologist. He knew we were interested in collecting and classifying the marine shells found there, and said he had branched out and was spending most of his time, and study, on the liguas, those beautifully colored, banded tree snails found on the smooth-barked trees in the hammocks throughout the Everglades. The hammocks are

those tree covered "islands" a few inches higher than the surrounding "seas" of saw grass.

At that time it was not against the law to collect liguas for private collections, except within The National Park. Our friend had made long, jointed bamboo poles that could be extended, one socketed into another, so that three lengths could reach twenty to twenty-five feet. The end section was equipped with a metal cup about two inches in diameter. During the winter months the liguas have finished their feeding on the lichens on the smooth-barked trees, and cement themselves, usually on the under side of a limb, with the small end pointing down.

To capture the liguas we would ride out some little trail in the Everglades, and park the car near the hammock we wanted to inspect. Then, holding a cluster of three sections of bamboo pole, we would slosh through muck six inches deep, avoiding the deeper pot holes, and break a way through saw grass six feet tall to the desired hammock. There you had to dodge around cactus, and through briars — with eyes turned upwards under the lisaloma and poison wood trees until you saw a ligua on the under side of a limb some twenty feet above you. Then, you joined the sections of bamboo together, to try to center the cup on the pole under the snail. If the wind was blowing, and the tree and pole were moving with the wind, this was often a very tedious and difficult procedure. Once contact was made, a wiggling of the pole usually loosened the snail and, taking the pole down, section by section, you deposited your captive in a little bag fastened on your belt. After getting your quota, you sloshed your way back, and if you had a

good sense of direction, finally found your car. It's
easy to get lost in the Everglades!!

Back at the lodge, after a good supper, you waited
until they were through in the kitchen and dropped
your "catch" in boiling water for three minutes. Then
with a pair of tweezers you carefully unwound the
animal from its shell — being very careful to get all of
the meat out, or you soon had a "stinker" that only
ants could clean out.

Different hammocks usually had snails with different colors and markings. In fact, in the early days of collecting liguas, we were told some of the natives used to collect all the liguas they could find on a hammock, then burn the hammock so there would be no more snails with that characteristic marking, so the price to the collectors would go up. On one of our expeditions, I got separated from our friend and found some unusually colored specimens. Our friend, who had taught us this fascinating hobby, swapped me a very fine and relatively rare junonia from deep in the Gulf of Mexico for one of those unusual liguas, and a day or so later confessed to me that at one of the "shell shops" the owner said he had just sold one like it to a collector for two hundred dollars! Still later he told us that he had tried to find his way back to the hammock where my unusual snail was found but couldn't find the place.

In the common dining room where all the guests ate supper together, there was a young family from Cincinnati with two little girls. The little girls were interested in the fact that I just wrote notes to people, and didn't talk. Their mother explained that I was a preacher and had paralyzed vocal chords and had to give my voice a complete rest. One of the little girls said, "Maybe the Lord didn't like what he was saying." Maybe so!!

Hazards of a Hillside Garden

Having moved to No. 2 Dogwood Circle, in the Warm Hearth Retirement community, in 1988, I found that most of the good garden spaces had been taken by earlier inhabitants. The only garden strip we could get was a ten-foot wide strip on the steepest part of the space left under the power lines. In this location anyone with the uncertain balance of a person my age always faces the problem of keeping from falling out of your garden and rolling down the hill. If you ended up lying on your back, you'd have a fellow feeling for a turtle stranded on its back. You are helpless until you can roll over and get to your knees, and then to your feet. And this is a difficult feat.

I usually carried a stout walking stick in one hand and often had a hoe in the other. They gave some measure of stability, until I saw a patch of weeds that needed slowing down with the hoe. Should I drop my stick to use the hoe, and come back to the stick after demolishing the offending weeds? That's what usually happened — but sometimes in reaching for the stick I would lose my balance and roll down hill farther than I intended.

At the bottom of the hill where the garden space ended there was a thick growth of ailanthus brush and weeds and briars. So I got permission to clean out all that stuff and extended my garden where this trash was growing. I transplanted a row of red raspberries from our old garden in town, and a row of asparagus — ditto; and some of Harry Mills' strawberries, which soon spread over quite an area. To protect this area from being rototilled or plowed under if and when the tiller came, I put up a twenty-foot section of fence for our green peas to climb on, to be followed by Kentucky wonder beans. But with my loss of a good sense of balance, picking peas I fell on my back in the strawberry patch. This did not help the berries, and the red stains on my back required a lot of explana-tions — such as; "No, my wife did not clobber me with the frying pan", or "No, I never served as a galley slave under the lash of a cruel taskmaster".

But my most embarrassing fall was several years ago when Mary Linda, and daughter Ruth, and I went out to the end of the Warm Hearth tract near the Linkous Cemetery. I knew there were a lot of black-berry thickets out there, along the ditch at the side of the alley leading to the Cemetery. A person's greedy nature is usually revealed in such a setting. I picked my spot across a roadside ditch and low fence oppo-site the patch of the biggest berries in sight. Then, leaning on my stick, I started reaching across the ditch and fence — but in leaning to get the biggest clump, I lost my balance and spun around so I fell on my back across the ditch and fence into the thickest part of the berry patch.

His wife and daughter heard him call;
In answer to his cries,
they tried to help him to his feet,
expressing great surprise.
But, head down and o'er a fence
he lay among the briars —
Like a turtle on its back — was he;
And thorns did scratch like fires.

His wife and daughter said
 he ought'er try to act his age.
Bit by bit he reached the stage
where he could turn and sit.
He pushed with stick — they pulled with hand,
 till with a heave he tried to stand —
and crawled away —
and vowed to stay from briar patches —
far away.

Gnats and Other Insects

As hurried and harried as life is today, few people take the time to notice and smell the flowers as they pass. Since retirement, with more leisure time to watch people, and other creatures both great and small, I never cease to marvel as I watch butterflies and hummingbird hawkmoths as they hover over the blooms on the budlia bush (butterfly bush) and uncoil their long, flexible tongues to suck nectar from the flowers. What wonderful agility is manifested as they hover, uncoil a long flexible tube, and insert it first in one bloom, and then another, with uncanny accuracy to suck up the nectar. It looks like more fun than watching a pretty girl sucking cider through a straw. If we had as accurate control of our tongues, it might be better for us, and for the world.

Although the honeybee does not display as delicate a dexterity, it more than earns its keep. Witness the care with which orchardists transport truck-loads of hives full of bees to different locations during the blooming season — apple orchards in the valley of Virginia, and orange groves in Florida when it's winter up here. These are not pleasure trips, like wealthy people take, but working trips.

How would you like to hand-pollinate an orchard of forty or a hundred acres of blooming apple trees, and then be trucked a thousand miles to do the same for citrus groves in Florida? And that's not to mention the gallons of honey you are expected to produce as a bonus contribution. We humans are probably more immediately aware of the sweet results than of the longer term results of their labors. Maybe there's a moral there also. Find it.

Maybe we should not throw into such stark contrast the wicked world of insect pests. We marvel at the beautiful and delicious gifts of our insect world, but we are plagued by the ever-present annoyance of other members of the same class.

Excuse me while I brush the gnats out of my eyes, ears, and nose, and off my neck. Now I can hear the mosquitoes buzz as they hunt for a good place to draw blood from a poor mortal. Those little musical critters do not exactly hum a tune we enjoy, but they at least warn you with a requiem you hate to hear. You hope it is for them — if you swat accurately — though it may be for you or me if they carry a lethal infection.

We do have some friends on our side. On a hot summer evening we used to like to lie on our backs on the lawn at dusk and watch the bats flying back and forth above us across the lawn with open-mouthed invitations for small insects to please enter for a hearty meal. Of course not specifying whose meal. Sometimes when we were in a teasing mood, we would toss up from where we lay on the lawn small hemlock cones and watch the bats catch the cones and of course drop them immediately. What remarkable sonars bats must have.

Of course there are even smaller denizens of the tribe in the wild blue yonder that seem to like to amuse themselves by making us itch. We will not elaborate on that, but return to the beauty of the butterflies — one of the symbols of immortality. Amen!

Steps

As kids, when we were sent upstairs to bed when company was coming, we often just sat on the top step, to see who it was, and what it was they were talking about. It might have been about something we had done — or failed to do — especially if it were one of our teachers, or a neighbor. That top step was a wonderful observation post where we often received warnings of dire consequences that lay in our futures. It also was a place where we learned not only of impending punishment — but also of promised rewards.

As kids, there was also a game we sometimes played of stepping on each other's shadows. This was far less dangerous and painful than actually stepping on each other. You could use all sorts of dodges from the one trying to step on your shadow, by getting in the shade of a tree — or by a sudden stop, or crouch, or by jumping to one side.

After we graduated from the old "Model T" to the "Model A" — with the foot control button for the accelerator on the floor of the car, to step on it meant to step harder on that floor button to go faster. In time, to "Step on it" just meant

to speed up — get a move on, you — stir your stumps.

As a cadet at Virginia Polytechnic Institute in 1921 in the ROTC — it was "catch step Rat — you are in the army now — you are not behind a plow" (the expurgated next line "from digging a ditch, you'll never get rich; you're in the army now." Steps. There was the riddle). "How far is it to London town? One foot up and one foot down. That's the way to London town." Steps. One step at a time.

In more recent times — a forceful command from the stern teacher Miss Wormwood to Calvin: "You step right down to the Principal's Office and tell him I sent you." It was a step that often led to painful results. The "Two Step" was something else. I never did fully master it.

Some of us old-timers remember when there were stepping stones across Main Street in Blacksburg to get across the two open creeks that crossed the street. If you missed, or slipped on one of these stepping stones and fell in the mud, you were sent to your room to change your wet and muddy things, and clean up for supper.

When Spring finally comes — as close to St. Patrick's day as possible, stake out your potato rows two steps apart, then a row, one good step further for a row of onions — close enough — so the onions would make the potatoes' eyes water. This would eliminate any need for ever watering. When the bugs begin to enjoy the leaves on the spuds or tomatoes, a form of non-toxic repellent is to step on the critters — that converts them into squash bugs, and is far less harmful to the environment.

Yes, Steps are wonderful places. You can sit there and watch the world go by. But your reverie is spoiled when someone higher up the chain of command says: "Step lively there, we haven't got all day." And our professor reminds us that to solve most problems, the first STEP is to define your terms, and your next STEP is to decide where you go.

In the meantime, your STEPson has found the STEPladder and is reaching for the cookie jar on the top shelf in the pantry.

You had better follow in Dad's footSTEPS and do what Mom says, or you will have to take the consequences.

STEPS play an important part in life.

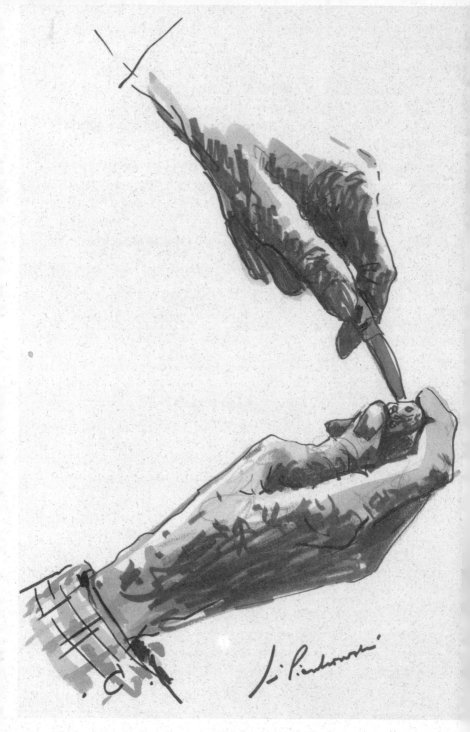

Perils of the Amateur

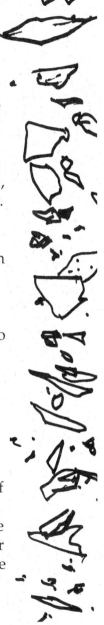

There are always stories of the city slicker who moves to the country to enjoy the free and easy and gracious life of the open spaces. The idea of planting a little garden and raising a few of his favorite vegetables leads to the planting of a row of butter-beans. Lo, and behold, the stupid things come up upside down. A neighbor, wishing to have a little fun, tells him that he planted the seed the wrong way and he will have to dig them up and turn them over. Furthermore, says the helpful neighbor, it's a good thing in that area to plant a row of onions alongside of a row of potatoes, so the onions will make the potatoes eyes water. Then he won't have to water the garden during the dry weather.

There is also the Mr. Fixit who fails to turn the electric switches off before working on the ceiling light, and he is shocked off the stool on which he is standing. When he recovers, he turns off all the switches in the junction box, and after finishing his job he fails to turn one of the switches back on. A few days later when his wife opens the deep freeze, she is nearly overcome by the terrible odor of the now spoiled meat they had carefully put in the deep freeze. His wife calls the salesman where they got the freezer. He sends a trained electrician, who comes and simply turns the switch back on, but charges her for making a house call.

Then there was a man who gave a friend some of his left-over expensive pills that had cured him of what he thought was a similar ailment. When the autopsy was performed on his friend, he narrowly escaped going to the electric chair. But, since it was done without malice aforethought, they just slapped a big fine on him and a jail sentence for practicing medicine without a license.

During the open season on deer, there are always a few amateur hunters who do not know that a gun is always loaded and should never be pointed at anything you do not intend to kill. "I didn't know it was loaded" is poor compensation for the death or wounding of another person.

There is usually someone from down South where ponds seldom freeze over thick enough on which to skate. On moving further north, he sees how beautifully a practiced skater spins and cuts his figures on the ice. He decides it looks like so much fun he buys a pair of skates. Even the children are skating with ease and grace. He does not take into account the fact that most skills that look so easy are acquired by much practice and many falls. When he launches out, though, the ice has suddenly become diabolically slick and hard. More than his pride is bruised — not only by his fall, but by his inability to get back up on his feet. Even his ankles and feet betray him. He concludes, correctly, that most skills that look so easy are the result of much practice, and the possession of certain physical characteristics.

The foibles and failures of amateurs are innumerable, but there are also unexpected successes that ought to encourage us to attempt new skills. A seventy-year-old woman decided she would take up something new every year to stimulate both mind and body. She enrolled in a Karate class for exercise and self assurance, and achieved a yellow belt. More important, she got the respect and obedience of troublesome small boys.

More surprisingly, she enrolled in a correspondence course in fiddle playing. It did not deter her that when she went into her back room to try "Home, Sweet Home," her two cats did not agree, and fled for the cat hole in the back door to escape...their "home sweet home".

Moral — if any!!! Do not be intimidated by the experts and professionals — cut loose and do something new for your own enjoyment and satisfaction.

Ice Storm — Post Mortem

I hope that I shall never see
Another ice storm break a tree
and scatter broken pines around
our yard — like a battle ground
of splintered trees and scattered trash.
But that gives work for you and me
to clean it up.

And you can see the exercise is good;
and you can bet
costs less than using "gyms"
and pedal bikes that you can get —
that take you nowhere, but make you sweat.

In Defense of Hieroglyphics

We have a son-in-law who is a re-
spected linguist in the field of Aramaic
and kindred Sumerian manuscripts and
cuneiform studies, but he has great
difficulty reading my letters to them. I
can understand that, because I often
have to ask my wife if she can make out
the notes I scribble in my "date book."

Recently we were baffled by a pre-
scription written by a highly educated
physician. Fortunately druggists are
either experts in the field of cryptogra-
phy — or they just look at the
physician's letterhead and phone him
for a translation of his secret code.

There have always been some people
who claim to be able to size up a
person's character either by looking at
their desk, or by a study of their hand-
writing. I am not alarmed by that. A
clear desk is often an indication that the
owner doesn't do much serious work;
and hand-writing is deceptive, because
many of the world's most gifted people
have never mastered the Spencerian
hand. Some lawyers, business officials,
and politicians studiously develop a
signature that no one can make out so
that they cannot be held accountable for

what they have written. Some of our most brilliant scientists and scholars stick to cursive script — rightly so called, as it leads to cursing when others try to read it — and it saves them time better employed in their field of study.

The typewriter was supposed to remedy the problem of legibility. However, I find that my old Remington doesn't know how to spell, and the blurr key is grossly overused, the margins are ragged and uneven, and the ribbon is always worn out, and the letters are struck with varied intensity — or missed altogether.

There is some justification in encouraging the younger generation to use that new-fangled gadget, the computer, that corrects spelling, strikes the keys with mechanically perfect intensity, maintains perfect margins, and is unmistakably legible. Although it is easy to read, it reminds me of the story about the Scottish "sermon taster". When asked how he liked a candidate's sermon, he replied, "I didna like it, for three reasons. In the fur-r-rst place, he r-r-read his sarmon. In the second place, he didna r-r-read it ver-r-a well. And in the thirrrd place, it wasna wurrth the r-r-reading". So much for legibility.

There may be some place for preserving the use of cursive script. It leaves more room for the reader's imagination, which is too often sadly lacking in our highly mechanized, literalistic, prosaic age.

If It Could Talk

What tales it could tell — if It could talk. It has six legs and sometimes flies. It is not an insect; it has had an important place in our family life for parts of four generations. It has been a focal point in the eating habits of our family and has served as a slaughter ground for creatures like flies and ants. Originally it was part of a consortium of specimens of *Quercus alba*, before being murdered and sawn asunder and worked upon by numerous artisans before winding up as a valued part of our family life.

Having survived so long it has achieved a patina hard to duplicate. In spite of numerous sandings, scrubbings, and waxings — it is still a marvel of survival.

It has had to listen to many childish quarrels, and parental corrections and threats. It has been bathed with tears, and resounded with laughter; shared good stories, excuses, and plans for family events. It has shared in visits from cousins, aunts, uncles, neighbors and friends. Very few secrets were unknown to it. It has been a focal point for departures to various distant places

— and for many glad homecomings. Many of our neighbors have shared its ample size — both for food, and for games. Dozens of V.P.I. Cadets were made part of the family group after church services. Small children used its cavernous space underneath for cabins, choo-choo trains, dragon caves and bomb shelters. Quarrels have been brewed and resolved around it. Turkeys, ducks, chickens, and porkers' quarters have been sacrificed on it. So here's to our durable, and versatile dining room table. Long may it survive.

Whatchamaycallit

Now that Webster's Dictionary has bowed to the inevitable, that "ain't" ain't no longer an outcast, but has been admitted to the family of proper words, and so is included in Webster's latest edition, I would suggest that they go a step further and recognize the usefulness and legitimacy of the word:

"WHATCHAMAYCALLIT."

Purists may want to use hyphens, thus "What-You-May-Call-It." Any way you may slice it, it adds up to the same thing.

To those of us who were born too long ago, this is a most useful word. It can be pronounced carefully, or just mumbled, and serves the same purpose either way. It can indicate either a total memory lapse, or a gap filler while you fish around for a word or name you cannot recall. Like when you want to introduce someone to a dear and long-time intimate friend and for the life of you the right name will not come out — maybe you can remember the first name, and you can sort of mutter a muffled — "I'm sure you must know whatchamacallit" — and camouflage this with a half smothered cough — or if

you are a country bumpkin, and in the correct setting, a squirt of tobacco juice can fill the vacuum.

That word is particularly useful when someone asks the name of one of the flowers in the yard — you can just say, "O, that is one of Mary Linda's whatchamaycallits; She will be glad to give you the Latin name when she comes out."

As a multi-hobbiest, it doesn't bother me at all when someone asks what is the name of that blue gem stone — I just reply, "I am not a geologist — but that's found in the desert of western Chihuahua, Mexico — I think it's a whatchamaycallit. I just cut and polished it." Seeing a beautifully polished slice of dark wood: "We cut that piece from a brush fence near Zacatecas in the high desert country — it's called a whatchamaycallit — I can't read what I put in my logbook — but I remember quite vividly when and where I got it."

Things reach a more critical point when it comes to planting our vegetable garden. Where did you plant the yellow squash? "O, it's next to that row of whatchamacallits. I just didn't have a pencil and paper with me to mark it." Now, the tomatoes are easy to identify. They are all in those wire cages. There are the Big Boys, Better Girls, Ponderos and a new hybrid called whatchamaycallit — I just don't recall the names of these hybrids.

But I planted a row of potatoes next to the onions — so the onions will make the potatoes' eyes water, and I won't have to irrigate them.

Now don't ask me what you call that. I think it's a WHATCHAMAYCALLIT.

Just Peanuts

(Congolese — Ngooba)

A common expression we often use in a disparaging way — "O that's just peanuts" — referring to something as being of no consequence. It now represents value in the millions of dollars annually.

There is a high probability that the peanut, or ground nut, came to this country smuggled in as a hitch-hiker on the person of Black slaves from the African Congo section, where it is indigenous. Surreptitiously raised in little private patches by slaves, it spread among the slaves in the Black Belt of the southern states. Raised in little hidden patches until finally some of the "red necks" found how good they were, and goober peas became a part of the diet of poor folks.

In a garden or field, the planting of peanuts seems to be such a foolish thing. The plant itself acts so irresponsibly. Just a bunch of green leaves, with remarkable pea-like leaves and flowers; overshadowed by bold, upstanding lilies, with resplendent colors, and amid so many beautiful flowers!! That was enough to make the obscure peanut

flowers hang their heads — ashamed to add so little of beauty to the garden scene. So the peanut flower just hung its head in shame and tried to hide its head down in the ground. But down there in the dark earth it seemed to say to itself — maybe I can't wear the beautiful dresses of the other garden flowers, but I will just see what I can do in the dark. Down there in the dirt where no one could see or criticize, it started doing its "thing". The little flowers that had gone under-ground in shame began to say among them-selves that although we cannot compete with the resplendent beauty of the many-colored blooms around us, we will see what we can do with what we have. With the strength of their united purpose and pride of being able to unite their efforts, they began to swell up and together formed a food chain now worth millions. Have some peanut brittle!!

Drat That Fly

Musca domestica, that all-too-common species of Diptera, known as the common housefly, has finally been diminished by the death of one specimen. This particular specimen had the nerve to light on my nose when I was trying to get my greatly needed afternoon nap. It was not at all disturbed by that old Civil War rhyme; "Shoo fly don't bother me — for I am a private in Company E." I was forced to resort to sterner measures. Cupping one hand, I decided to catch the offending creature and break every bone in its body. I only succeeded in bloodying my nose and jabbing my thumb in my eye.

DRAT THAT FLY!

The creature merely flew to the table — where we had just finished breakfast — while I was reading the newspaper — all about the bloodshed in so many un-pronounceable places, and hopefully now on our dining room table, as with a folded newspaper I carefully stalked the vicious creature. I could only be charged with premeditated murder if my plot succeeded, and attempted murder if my plans failed to capture, punish, mutilate,

squash, and otherwise frustrate the obnoxious behavior of poor misguided specimen of the Diptera. Taking careful aim, I swung at the creature — but only succeeded in knocking the milk pitcher and honey dish to the floor. If you never tried to get honey out of a rug, don't!

Just hang the thing out in the yard for the bees, ants, and yellow jackets. They can do a better job than we mortals can ever accomplish. Then throw the sticky thing away.

DRAT THAT FLY !!

The peace and quiet of our usually calm family life is now shattered. The fly is still enjoying its freedom, and is feasting from the remains of the breakfast it has scattered. But this specimen of Homo sapiens is determined not to surrender. Going to the corner of the room where my father kept his arsenal of lethal weapons — I decided not to use his double-barreled shotgun, pistol, or Winchester rifle, and chose an apparently harmless thing — a butterfly net. It had a good stout handle and, as I swung around, the handle struck a full-length mirror on the bathroom door. Broken glass on a bathroom floor spells trouble for somebody. .

DRAT THAT FLY !!!

With net in hand, I felt that I was more than a match for any number of flies. But as I turned from the broken glass on the bathroom floor, the net somehow got tangled with a row of potted geraniums on the window ledge, and they came crashing down — and great was the fall thereof! Added to the broken

mirror there was now broken pottery, and enough potting soil to grow flowers sufficient to cover my grave. Woe is me!!

DRAT THAT FLY!!!!

Bloodied, but unbowed, I raised up on one elbow and saw a can of "Raid". Although strongly opposed to resorting to chemical warfare, with that can I did spray, and then I did pray, and thought I would die with that pesky old fly.

DRAT THAT FLY!

Jaundiced Reflections

Every profession needs deflating
from time to time: the butcher, the
baker, the candlestick maker, the physician, the clergy, the lawyers, the politicians — you name them, I've got them
on my list.

Now, with malice towards none, and
charity towards all, and with tongue in
both cheeks, let's begin with that profession with which we both begin and end
life - the medical profession. As I sat
waiting, waiting, WAITING, he finally
bounced in and cheerfully asked:
"What's the matter this time? According
to your chart, your blood pressure
indicates that your heart is still beating.
Your temperature is a little below the
boiling point. Open your mouth wide
and stick out your tongue while you tell
me what you had for breakfast. Let me
check your reflexes [as he hits your knee
with a sledge hammer]. Breathe deeply
now and hold it while I answer the
telephone and while you stand on one
foot. Now the other one. You say you
are troubled with post-nasal drip. The
only sure cure for that is decapitation
(ha, ha). Some people who have had
that treatment have complained after-

wards that the treatment was worse than the problem. Have you tried gargling with fuming nitric acid? DON'T. I notice some evidence of hypobolic fluctuations of your occipital transistor. We may have to remedy that by a radical excision of the polygonial whangdoodle of your epiglottis. Did your maternal grandfather ever show any signs of this type of disorder? What did he die of? Why: What color were his eyes? Both of them? This may be hereditary, you know. I would recommend that you cut out tea, coffee, buttermilk, and arsenate of lead. Likewise, chewing and smoking tobacco; or pernicious lepidoptera may develop in the left ventricle of your transmogrifier. Take one of these $15 sugar pills three times a day. They will help me more than they will you. At the desk, make an appointment to see me again in a week if you survive my treatment. You may leave your check at the cashier's window as you pass out. Have a good day."

Now let's take a look at the clergy:
Being one of them myself, I may have a prejudicial view of this strange breed. I bite my tongue as I try to hold it in my other cheek. Clergymen come in odd shapes and sizes, but there are a number of distinct types. Some are very pompous for, after all, haven't they been called by God to speak for Him. That's a very serious business and a solemn and dignified mein is necessary in order to impress the lesser breeds with one's divine importance. It helps if you can prefix your name with a high-sounding title like, "The Very Reverend, or The Most Reverend, or Arch-

bishop" or something equally impressive. Anyway you slice it, an inflated ego is very apt to ensue.

There is another very different type — the backslapping, "hail fellow well met" who hobnobs with the "man upstairs," who after all is a pretty good old guy, if you don't take his religion too seriously.

Somewhat akin to this type is the one who thinks he is being paid to be an entertainer. Don't bother with any serious theology — he never has time for that stuff. Just tell enough funny tales and a few jokes to get people laughing — add a sob story or two as clinchers and you have got them. Your salary will go up or down depending on the decibel rating on the laugh scale, or the number of wet handkerchiefs, either from tears or laughter.

At the other extreme is the super-orthodox, studious type who is immersed in the theological tomes in his study, and is invisible to the congregation six days a week — and is incomprehensible on the seventh, when he stands in the pulpit to preach.

Then there is the doorbell ringer. Watch and pray, for you know not what time of day or night he cometh.

There is also the cult that measures godliness by "busy-ness". Keep the sheep so busy with meetings of all sorts, they won't have time to "sin," then you will have more time for golf.

Among the "unmentionables" are the money-grubbing televangelists who corrupt the airwaves and the gullible public. To quote the old spiritual: "Everybody talkin 'bout Heaven ain't a-going there."

There are others: The Bible thumpers, shouters, foot stompers and, at the other extreme, the whisperers, who think they can convince people they are being given very profound esoteric truth by whispering. Barnum was conservative when he said, "A sucker is born every minute."

But one common weakness which afflicts most of us is in taking ourselves too seriously. Take God and His gift of life seriously — but not one's self. We are all of the same common clay. Thank God when it is possible to practice a few of the things we all too glibly profess. And that goes for all of us.

What about the legal profession?

Some of my kinfolks and best friends are of that ilk. Just as in any area of life, you find the money grubbers, and charlatans. Mark Twain recommended hanging all lawyers. But if that happened, our language would be greatly impoverished. For after all, who can use more obscure words to confuse simple ideas than lawyers? Someone has said that language is the means by which people misunderstand each other. It might be the task of lawyers to explain the unexplainable and unscrew the inscrutable. But no. Their language is so broken up with the wherever as, on the other hand, the party of the first part, non compos mentis, not to mention exnihilo fit and nox vomica — with E pluribus unum to boot. It takes a Philadelphia lawyer to cut through the excess verbiage, and confuse you with his own set of incomprehensibles. Lawyers really have the public behind the eight ball. It takes a lawyer to understand another lawyer. So once you are involved with the law, there is no escape — until you pay for it.

As for the politician ...

He knows that in order to get elected, he must promise everybody everything and kiss all the runny-nosed, wet-bottomed babies and old women. Tell enough jokes, press the flesh every chance he gets. Go where the voters are. Downgrade his opponent and deride his past record. In answer to any question, always respond: "That's a very good question. I am going to answer that in detail in my speech at our fundraising dinner tonight. You be there." (Admission $25). Criticize your opponent's negative campaign and the lies put out by his propaganda staff. Ring the changes on your loyalty to the flag, apple pie and motherhood. Quote, or misquote if necessary, the "Founding Fathers" to line them up on your side. Lambaste communism, terrorism, drug racketeers, crime. Come out strong for education, national defense, good weather, good health, good roads — Good grief! Promise to cut taxes, cut government, cut red tape. Get a good staff of public relations experts. Have lots of photos of yourself in favorable settings. Get your speech writers to find favorable quotes from famous sources — even if they have to make them up. Adapt your dress and manner of speaking to suit the people in the area where you are speaking. Always be ready to say, "I have been misquoted by the media. What I really said was (whatever they wanted to hear), when I am elected, things will be different, Thank you, goodbye, God bless you, and have a nice day — and be sure to vote for me."

Feathered and Featherless Bipeds

Apparently neither of these types like to be listed as numbers instead of by names. Yet there are important facts to be gleaned from listing them by numbers. For instance, how many mouths need to be filled in Somalia, and how many tons of food are needed.

While I was writing this, a flight of around one to two hundred sea gulls flew over Warm Hearth heading East. They often come inland when the corn fields have just been harvested. Question? Were they just interested in freshly exposed protein in the form of worms and bugs?; Or were they eating fallen grain? — Or maybe they were just flying from one garbage dump to another. They have had their natural feeding habits affected by human behavior and misbehavior — what featherless bipeds throw out. There we have both names and numbers.

The day I started writing this was the day of the official bird count in the Blacksburg area. As so often happens, this usually comes when we have very unsettled weather conditions. It was a great day, cold with Scotch mist. Our feathered bipeds had more sense than

1937

the featherless variety, and remained strictly under cover. Not a single bird came to our feeder all day. The same was true at the feeders of several friends. Several of the younger and more venturesome, or stupid, members of our bird club did get out, as we used to do when we were also younger and maybe more stupid. They reported a fair number of birds. In fact the total count of species for the day approached the average of around 80 species.

Of course, the next day was clear and our feeder was running over with all our usual feathered friends.

SO WHAT! AND WHY?

You do not have to be an Ornithologist and scientist to find excuses for being considered a freak, or a harmless sort of idiot, sloshing around in all sorts of weather with bird glasses and a pad, counting the birdies. Birds are an important part of the same web of life to which we belong. Fluctuations in their distribution help to verify, and sometimes predict, climatic changes that affect us all. They can sometimes confuse or nullify predictions based on other events. They can inspire us with their beauty — which is its own reward. Eight bluebirds in our dogwood tree in our front yard eating the red berries present a picture no human artist can exceed.

Our asparagus bed in the garden is the free gift of birds that planted the seed, together with fertilizer, and no toxic chemicals were ever used. Every year as I work in our garden I have good reason to be thankful for our feathered co-workers. Although the robins do get a fair share of the best strawberries, the birds more than pay their way by all the bugs and weed seeds they eat. Their help does not impose a hazard to our environment, either.

In a community like Warm Hearth with several hundred elderly people, it is interesting to see how many of the people here have put out feeders and bird boxes. WHY? They are a source of interest and delight that older folks can enjoy and appreciate with very little expense or effort.

Birds also exhibit so many of the weaknesses and foibles of the featherless biped, such as greed and jealousy, that they can help fulfill Robert Burns' prayer: "O wad some power the giftie gie us, to see ourselves as others see us. It would from many a blunder free us, and foolish notion." (With apologies for an anglicized version and thanks for the birds.)

Transplanting

This year, in a burst of idealistic zeal,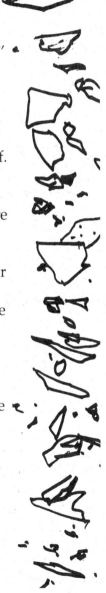
and to show some practical concern for
Mary Linda's back, which had caused
some painful reaction from stooping so
much to transplant bunches of seedling
lettuce to more spacious room in the
garden, I decided to do the work myself.
This was also a remonstrance to my
prodigal waste of seed by pouring too
many seeds into too small a space. There
was the not-so-subtle reminder that
seeds cost money, and should not be
wasted. Both Benjamin Franklin and our
Calvinistic ethic coincided in the belief
that a penny saved could be put to more
constructive use than wasting lettuce
seed.

Good resolutions do not always
work. This year the lettuce seeds be-
haved as usual. They tumbled out of the
envelope in a pile to do what seeds are
supposed to do. They must have
achieved at least 150% germination.
They all sprouted and crowded each
other for living space.

I was elected to do something about
it. Taking the hoe, I cleared out the row
where we wanted them to grow, and

poured on the water. Rain was predicted for the next day, which sounded like a made-to-order command to transplant those crowded lettuce plants. Right after breakfast I started putting my good resolutions into effect. Armed with a jug of water, foam rubber pad, and a plastic container full of seedling lettuce plants, I limped towards my Armageddon.

Dropping the kneeling pad where I thought I could reach the most plants, I was faced with a momentous decision with important theological dimensions. Having retired from the active Pastorate twenty-five years ago, I was confronted with a soul-testing decision. If I had been a Romanist or even an Episcopalian, kneeling on the foam rubber pad would have been the only position for setting out the seedling plants. But the long tradition of the Reformed Church was to kneel to no earthly power — king, tyrant, or lettuce seedlings. Long tradition decrees that we either stand or sit for prayer — and certainly, setting out seedling lettuce plants calls for prayer and the use of many theological terms not usually associated with prayer.

I worked out a compromise between sitting and standing. I sat on the pad with legs stretched out across the prepared trench for the seedlings. I could reach both to right and left and got along fine until I had reached as far as possible in both directions. Then the problem was to move my carcass to a new spot further down the line. With nothing to hold to, I still managed a most un-ministerial hip wiggle, and got to a position further down the trench.

After completing that transplanting area, it was time to get on my feet to a standing position — which

was quite in keeping with my theological convictions,
but for the life of me I could not get to my feet, without having something to pull up by. Could I roll over
on my knees? Would that violate my theological
convictions? I swallowed hard, prayed for forgive-
ness, and suddenly remembered that I had helped to
lead certain Ecumenical meetings, where we often
followed the practice of the cooperating churches.
That gave me a measure of comfort as I rolled over to
my knees, and was able to stand. Amen and Hallelu-
jah.

Beyond the Cashier's Desk

It used to be such a pain in the foot and back to have to stand in line at the cashier's desk while some dear old soul fished around in a voluminous shopping bag for her checkbook, then for her pen. Then for her copy of the bill she owed that she could not read without her glasses. Then she had to hunt for her glasses that were securely pinned to her dress. Then she had to empty out her shopping bag to see if she had put her bill in there. Then put the stuff back in her bag when some kind person told her that her glasses were pinned to her dress. Then she had to empty her bag again to find her copy of her bill.

Now at a more advanced age myself, I can suffer with her as I go through similar antics myself. Emptying one pocket after another in search of that elusive bill and then for the pocketbook to pay for same. Emptying one pocket after another and finally paying, but on the way out of the store turning back to see if I had missed anything. As I start for the door one of my bags splits and bird seed is scattered all over the floor. As a janitor advances with a mop and dustpan, he backs into an aquarium full of gold fish on a little table near the door and spreads half a dozen gold fish gasping on the floor. The janitor has to warn people not to slip on the wet floor or step on the poor gasping gold fish.

You have to take the bus home since you cannot drive the car anymore. Meanwhile, the janitor has been busy mopping up the floor and has hurriedly picked up the goldfish and put them in a plastic bag of water which he has put in your hands to hold.

In the meantime, your bus has come and you are pushed into it, still holding the plastic bag of water with the goldfish. No one will accept the bag of gold fish when they shove you into the bus, and the driver most emphatically says that you can't take the bag of gold fish into the back of the bus — leave the bag on the corner of the step until you get off. But at the next stop a big-footed policeman steps on the bag of un-wanted gold fish and they are squeezed out all over the front of the bus. The cop tells the driver he will be arrested if he doesn't mop up the mess and warn passengers about the wet floor.

As you get off the bus, you half turn and say to the driver —

HAVE A NICE DAY!

Locked In
(a prisoner in your own home)

The other morning I was performing
the usual duties, such as setting the
table, cooking grits, and trying to decide
which we should have — canned
salmon, tuna, sausage, egg beaters or
bacon (anything goes well with grits).
Then wash the poison off the grapefruit,
pour the blue john, put the 100% coffee
in the microwave, put bread in the
toaster, ready to burn it; then apple
sauce, jelly and some kind of yellow
grease - given the honorary title of
butter. Now collapse in my chair with
the newspaper and turn to Calvin and
Hobbes to give a ray of hope for the
beginning of a new day. You can skim
hurriedly through the blood and gore
that is served up as news, and hurriedly
scan the "yo-yo" stock report.

Then in answer to the beseeching
appeals of the birds and squirrels, I take
a bag of sunflower seeds and try to go
out the back door. But the dad-burned
lock has sprung and I cannot open the
door. I am locked in my own house.
Alice and the White Queen remind me

that there is surely a moral there — locked in my own small house.

I forget what poet it was who said, "We build too low who builds below the stars," and I also have a vague recollection of another third-grade episode where we read about an idiotic youngster who was trying to peddle excelsior, or some other type of wood fiber, up in the Alps as he tried to reach the mountain top. He ought to have been locked in his house, or the lunatic asylum. But what about getting out of my house? I have a nice protective cover. I ought to be content to let the rest of the world go by-to perdition, for all I care; why bother to open the door?

But the truth is, the world will not just quietly pass by. It may leave us in peace — or in pieces. The world is still a dangerous place — even in America. There are many kinds of death, and physical death, though sure in the end, may not be either the most common or painful.

We are so prone to lock ourselves up in too small an environment, while the whole wide world is ours, for those with the eyes and imagination to see.

There is a microcosm or world of small things that we overlook, or fail to take into account, and I don't mean just germs. For instance, there was the little girl who longed for the loving companionship of her mother, who was so active in adult concerns — not necessarily the bridge club but taking part in legitimate activities designed to improve the health and well-being of their entire community. But the little girl was hungry for mother-loving companionship and concern — "Mummy can you spare me some time to help me make some cookies for our friends?" Or the little boy whose father has just returned from a frustrating day at the office: "Daddy, here's the nice ball you gave me. Could we play catch together a few minutes before supper?"

Little things — little people. How often we miss the golden opportunity to share in a child's world again. And as time passes, the gap widens until it's too late to build bridges of understanding and kindness. Nothing is just a petty annoyance if it leads to the neglect of little people — either small in physical size or people who have had little opportunity to develop their latent abilities.

I was not even aware of the possibilities locked up in Johnnie's life. He lived out beyond Tom's Creek on the edge of the mountain. It is interesting how one thing leads to another. I had been out later than usual one afternoon and the winding country road between the creek and the mountain demanded close attention. Then the car started missing on one cylinder and then stopped. I used to be able to fix a Model "T" — sometimes with a piece of wire carefully borrowed from a roadside fence, or hay bale. But when I raise the hood on one of these new-fangled cars, and see the complicated gizmos crammed in the engine's gizzard, I just shut the hood down and hunt for help.